I0060662

ENTREPRENEUR
DAD

7 KEYS

TO A
SUCCESSFUL
BUSINESS
AND A HAPPY
FAMILY LIFE

JEFF
LOPES

Entrepreneur Dad: 7 Keys to a Successful Business and a Happy Family Life

Copyright © 2021 by Jeff Lopes. All rights reserved.

No part of this book may be reproduced in any form or by any mechanical means, including information storage and retrieval systems without permission in writing from the publisher/author, except by a reviewer who may quote passages in a review.

All images, logos, quotes, and trademarks included in this book are subject to use according to trademark and copyright laws of the United States of America.

ISBN: 978-1-64775-281-1

SELF-HELP / Personal Growth / Success

Cover and Interior design by Victoria Wolf, wolfdesignandmarketing.com

All rights reserved by Jeff Lopes.

Printed in the United States of America.

There are only two days in the year that nothing can be done. One is called yesterday, and the other is called tomorrow. Today is the right day to love, believe, do, and mostly live.

—Dalai Lama

CONTENTS

CHAPTER 1

REDEFINING
SUCCESS

ENTREPRENEURS WANT to change lives. I hear it every day from a new entrepreneur who says, "I want to have a positive impact on a thousand people. A hundred thousand. A million." I love it. It's a big part of why I'm an entrepreneur myself, and it's why I derive such satisfaction from helping entrepreneurs maximize their success.

When I'm coaching entrepreneurs to grow their businesses, one of the first things I do is hold an information-gathering session. This serves two functions: It helps us build a rapport, and it gives me an understanding of their story. Everyone has a story, and I can only help entrepreneurs get to where they want to go when I understand where they have been and where they are now. During these sessions, the first questions I ask are these: "Are you happy? Is your family happy?" Before the entrepreneur answers, he often hesitates, for fear of what the truth may be or what I might think of that entrepreneur. A frightening amount of the time, the answer is no.

The entrepreneurs who came before us, our fathers and grandfathers, taught us a model wherein success was equal to time and effort. They owned hardware stores and butcher shops, and by pulling long hours, some of them managed to grow their businesses through sheer effort alone. Many never grasped the true meaning of being wealthy; to many, wealth was measured in materialistic items, not freedom. This model of thinking doesn't work at *all* for entrepreneurs with families today; it only kind of worked for those who came before us. Yet so many continue in their footsteps.

You can be both a successful entrepreneur and an involved family member. In fact, you must be both—for the sake of your family *and* your business. To all entrepreneurs who are fathers (whom I'll refer to hereafter as entrepreneur-dads), I challenge you to let go of the old way of thinking about entrepreneurship and the limiting beliefs you might not know you're holding.

Let's look at four common limiting beliefs or myths that lead men to put their business above their family.

MYTH #1:
YOUR BUSINESS IS YOUR BABY

There is danger in letting your entrepreneurial drive and ambition go unchecked. By focusing too intensely on professional goals, entrepreneurs often develop blinders to more important things—that are, health, family, and overall happiness. In their determination, they make business their number-one purpose, and in so doing, relegate everything else to a secondary priority at best.

The effects of this myopia can be devastating. I've seen entrepreneur-dads so driven to start a business that they stop taking care of their bodies and develop serious health problems as a result. I've seen them put their families in precarious financial positions, investing everything they have in their business. I've seen their marriages fall apart because they have no time to connect with their spouses. I've seen them unwittingly neglect their kids, spending long hours working on the business until an entire childhood has come and gone.

Once I recognized the flaws in this way of thinking, it didn't just make the lives of my loved ones better—although that would've been enough. It also improved my business. By prioritizing my family, I forced myself to restrategize my entrepreneurship, building a more sustainable schedule and a stable source of income.

From a sustainability standpoint, I needed room in my schedule to be with my family and take care of myself. My workload made this impossible, so I fired myself from every role in my business that could stand to lose me, and I trained a team I could trust to take over. Not only did this give me the freedom to balance my schedule, but also it enabled my new team to bring the energy and ideas my business needed to grow.

Finding a healthy balance between family and business also helped me stabilize my financial position and actually earn more. Because business success can always go away, just as life and good health are never guaranteed, I needed another stream of income to ensure my children's financial security should the worst happen. With my hands already full with the commitments to my family and existing business, I knew that a new stream of income would have to be passive. With these as my parameters, I began to invest in the real estate market, and I built a second business, focusing my portfolio around vacation rentals. These vacation properties added a tremendous passive income, ensuring my family's financial future. This also enabled me to take greater risks with my business and invest more into growing each venture.

As an entrepreneur, you need to ask yourself how you will determine or measure success. To me, success is good health, loving family, and finance freedom. Once you figure out your honest vision of success, put that above everything else, and I promise you, entrepreneurial success will follow.

MYTH #2:
WEALTH IS MONEY

When I was nineteen years old, cutting my teeth as an entrepreneur in the fitness space, I met a man who epitomized my conception of entrepreneurial success. The man was worth millions. He owned a franchise of gyms. He lived in a hulking, O-shaped mansion with an Olympic-sized pool and a track at its center. He drove luxurious cars. He had the dream life of the entrepreneurs you read about in magazines. He'd hired my fitness-consulting business to help him sell personal training in his gyms, so there I was, a nineteen-year-old entrepreneur, working closely with him, hungry for the sort of wealth I saw before me.

However, as I got to know him through our work together, it became clear he was the loneliest person I'd ever met. He worked incredible hours, had next to no family life, and was deep in a depressive episode. Yes, he had a massive house, but only one other person lived in it—a member of the staff he'd hired to take care of the place. The man was almost always by himself, and when he was with other people, he was paranoid they were only around him for his money. In this way, even when he was with others, he was alone.

For me, it was an eye-opener. Here was an entrepreneur with all the money in the world, and he was miserable. Something clicked. Maybe I wanted the beautiful house, the glittering cars, and the fine clothes, but I didn't want to be that guy. There had to be a better balance to life.

Ever since then, there's been a voice in the back of my head that has reminded me that money is not a substitute for a meaningful life. Money is an engine that if used correctly can drive you to a wonderful life—once you find your purpose. If you don't enjoy your life or if you die lonely, what good is money in the bank? Have you ever seen a funeral procession with a money truck following it? I haven't.

Being wealthy is not about having money; it's about having the freedom to live the life you want. While the two are intertwined, they are far from the same. This is critical for an entrepreneur-dad to understand. The success of your business means nothing, if you don't have the freedom to enjoy it.

MYTH #3:
I'M DOING THIS ALL FOR THEM

When I ask busy entrepreneur-dads how much time they spend with their kids, their answer is almost always the same: "I'm doing this all for them." This has a certain logic to it. The money they bring in during their long, stressful hours at work will pay for their kid to go to college, have a new car when they turn sixteen, or wear the freshest clothes on the block.

It's clear from their body language; the entrepreneurs who tell me this don't fully believe it. They look defensive, cross their arms, and furrow their brows at me. In their minds, their work is a sacrifice they make for their family, which is admirable, but what their children truly need is their love and time. There is no substitute for quality time.

You don't have to look far for evidence. Every day, another celebrity's child checks into rehab. Their parents were never around and just fed them money to make up for it. Now as adults, they lack a strong foundation and live unstable lives as a result.

I cannot stress this enough: Children just want their parents to love them. Don't over-complicate it. They don't care how much money you have in your account, how nice of a house you live in, or if you can afford to buy them lots of toys. Yes, your child may grin ear to ear when you give him or her a new toy, but that smile is not there because of that toy. The child is smiling because of being with Dad and feeling his love. There is nothing more rewarding than when your child has a big win and you're there to be the first to give a hug.

MYTH #4: I WISH I HAD MORE TIME

When I speak with other entrepreneur-dads, they're often shocked to hear how much time I spend each day with my family (3 p.m. to 7 p.m. is family time). They shake their heads, and with a hint of jealousy lament the fullness of their schedules. If only they had more time, they say, they would be with their children. With more time, they could go visit their parents, who they've been meaning to see. They would take better care of themselves, get a full night's sleep, and exercise more—if only they had the time.

There is little that upsets me more than hearing the words "I wish I had more time." No one in all of human history has received more or less than twenty-four hours a day. We all have the time to be both successful entrepreneurs and involved family members. I guarantee it. If our schedules say otherwise, it's not a problem of hours in the day, but of priorities—how we are choosing to utilize our time.

When we're working these insane hours, focused on building this empire, stuck in the rhythm of nonstop work, it can be easy to grow numb to everything we're missing out on. The kids grow up; the spouse grows apart; the parents grow old. Days turn to months, months turn to years. Until one day something happens to a family member, and we realize how little time we've spent with that person. I've consoled entrepreneurs on the death of their parents, and all too often, they look at me, teary-eyed, and say, "I wish I'd had more time with them."

As much as I feel their pain, I can't help but feel frustrated. They *had* the time, they just didn't utilize it. If you have living family members, spend time with them while they're here. When is the last time you told your loved ones you loved them? Make it a habit; those simple words mean more than the world. Tomorrow is never guaranteed.

Money is the vehicle driving you to become successful. Freedom to do what you want, when you want, is your final destination.

CHAPTER 2

KIDS JUST WANT TO BE LOVED: LOVE IS OXYGEN

A FEW DAYS BEFORE our son was born, my wife caught a common virus. By a one-in-three-million chance, the virus passed from her to the baby. This resulted in a number of life-threatening complications, for both my wife and our child, and a chain of events that would change our family forever. The details of this are too great to go into here, but to make a long story short, when my son was born, he had a rare condition, and his odds of survival were very low. Due to this, he spent the first almost four months of his life at SickKids hospital in the ICU with five other sick babies.

As most parents would, or so I thought, my wife and I dedicated our lives to getting him home from the hospital. We turned off our houseline and our answering service, and we disconnected from the world. Every minute we could, we were with our son, usually from seven in the morning to six at night. Every day we had to rush home to pick up our daughter.

There was a high turnover rate in the fourth-floor ICU. Every few days, a new baby would appear in one of the beds, and when that happened, it meant the baby who'd been there before had passed away. It was hard to see the number of babies who passed through this tragic circle. What we did not see much of was their parents.

The months dragged on, and my wife and I showered our son with as much love as possible, savoring every moment of what we feared could be a very short life. But as we did, the silence of the other parents grew deafening. So many of their babies were dying alone, without the love and support they needed. Eventually, I had to ask one of the nurses, "Why are there rarely any other parents here?"

She told me, "Ninety percent of the children in this room aren't going to make it. Their parents know that, and they don't want to build a connection with a child they know they are going to lose. Your child's going to make it out of here because he knows you're here with him every day."

Even today, her words make me want to cry. Sometimes I'll catch myself thinking about how many of those kids might have survived if they'd had their parents by their side. If their parents had said, "I don't care if I only have six weeks with this baby. I'm going to spend those six weeks showing every bit of love I can to this child." I try not to brood over it. I'll never know.

What I do know is Tiago came home from the hospital and proceeded to shatter every lowered expectation the world placed upon him. I know he owes his success more than anything to himself, his ineffable qualities as a human being, his unstoppable drive. But I also know, without the love my wife and I poured over him in his first months, his life might have ended in the hospital. Love is like oxygen to children. They need it to survive and flourish. There is no substitute.

Most of the entrepreneurs I work with find this obvious—children need love—but will in the same breath demonstrate that they don't know *how* to give their children love. Knowing you love a child is one thing; showing it is another.

LOVE IS TIME

I speak with a lot of young entrepreneurs, whom I'm coaching or interviewing, and it's crazy—almost all of them have a story of redemption. The story is always so similar. They didn't have a relationship with their parents, or they blame them for not providing the stability they needed to have a "normal" childhood. As they grew up, this lack of foundation manifested in different ways—maybe a struggle with drugs, maybe legal trouble. What these manifestations all have in common is rebellion against their parents. And when these young entrepreneurs rebelled, their fathers didn't understand why.

However, if you ask their dads why their kids rebelled, I guarantee most will say the exact same thing: "I don't know. I gave my kids everything."

I've had many conversations like this with dads who have proven entrepreneurial success records and children leaning in the wrong direction. They usually direct me to the same conversation with that same refrain: "I gave my kids everything." They offer me proof, illustrating how much love they've given their children. Exhibit A—the car. Exhibit B—the Jordan sneakers. It's never 100 percent clear who he's trying to convince— me, himself, or his kid.

To be clear, having the financial freedom to buy stuff for your kids can be a great thing. Spoiling your child now and then *can* show the depth of your love. But many entrepreneur-dads forget that a gift is only worth as much to your child as the love you imbue it with. Intentional or not, giving a child a gift without the quality time and loving support to back it is the same as trying to buy their love. It's a cliché because it's true: you can't buy love.

At least twice a year, I take off work and spend a "Dad Day" with each of my respective children. I like to do one every few months, but I am always sure to spend such a day with them in the week surrounding their birthdays. We'll eat out, go shopping, and do whatever else strikes the birthday girl or boys fancy. It's a day of material gifts and, frankly, a ton of fun. My kids look forward to Dad Days, almost more than their actual birthdays, not because my daughter finds manicures all that euphoric or because my son's wildest dreams come true when I buy him a new baseball mitt, but because it's an entire day dedicated to the love between them and their dad. It's not the gifts; it's the love behind them and the time together that we cherish.

This is what I tell the fraught parent in my office. In the end, kids don't care about material things. They just want to be loved. Any child would gladly give up a new pair of Jordans sneakers if it meant playing basketball with his or her dad every day. A child who grows up in poverty with involved, loving parents will be much happier than a child who grows up surrounded in luxury but with absentees raising him or her. There is no replacement in a child's life for parental love, and the best way for a parent to show that love is quality time, the clock is ticking.

Roughly 80 percent of the face time we will spend with our children will be before the age of eighteen years old. How many of us realize that fact? Kids are only small for a small amount of time, beyond which a parent's relationship with that child becomes much harder to change Think of it as a piece of clay. When it's fresh out of the box, you can handle and mold it to any shape or form you wish. Once it starts to age and harden, it becomes much more difficult to mold. Show your children love by spending time together early and often, and by the time they're adults, you'll have a strong foundation of trust. If you show your love through gifts and gifts alone, don't be surprised if they grow distant and materialistic. As a parent of young children, you are teaching them what to expect of their relationship with you, and they learn *quickly*.

I am a strong believer in the Yes Factor. It's simple; if my kids ask me for anything surrounding spending time with them or helping them out, no matter what I am doing or how tired I am, I will do it. Earlier during this past week, I was sitting on the couch, half asleep, and my daughter said the Amazon Alexa in her room wasn't working and she couldn't watch Netflix. I could have easily said, "Hun, I will fix it in the morning." After all, I had just sat down for the first time after a long day. Instead, a voice came into the back of my head, and I got up, went upstairs, and reset everything and got it working.

The Yes Factor is there to show my kids I am always there to help them, with the hope that they will take that mindset into their adulthood and use it to say yes to help-ing others. Because my kids are young, this means always saying yes to spending quality time together. Just say yes. It doesn't matter how tired I am, if they ask me to do something with them, I'm doing it. At this moment in our relationship, they're eager to spend time with me, and their minds are developing lifelong patterns—and fast. This moment will only happen once.

By becoming fathers, we've made the decision to love our kids more than anything. To show that love in a way our children can actually feel, we have to *be* with them. Love takes time. Entrepreneurs have jam-packed schedules—believe me, I get it. If you don't see where you can fit in more time with your kids, it's time to build a new schedule.

The greatest
gift you
can ever give
your children
is belief in
themselves.

CHAPTER 3

MAKE TIME: PRIORITIZE AND SCHEDULE EVERYTHING

BEING AN ENTREPRENEUR should allow you to spend more time with your family than a nine-to-five job. This freedom is what drives many to become entrepreneurs in the first place. Yet most entrepreneurs end up working more hours and being more stressed than they would if they worked for someone else. This is 100 percent wrong. The cause? A disconnect from their purposes, poor prioritization, and lack of a schedule (or the discipline to adhere to one).

When an entrepreneur is missing this connection to purpose, priorities, and sticking to a schedule, he or she inevitably gets stuck at work. A meeting runs over, a project takes longer than expected, and tasks pile up. Soon the entrepreneur is missing out on family events and foregoing self-care. The common "I'll start working out tomorrow or next week" becomes a broken record, and health gets pushed to the side. Not only is this bad for business, it brings suffering on the family.

Your family, and *you*, deserve better. Building a routine that includes time for your family and you are the most important action you can take toward being a better entrepreneur, father, and person. It's not hard; the process is only three steps: set your purposes, prioritize, and schedule.

SET YOUR PURPOSES

Before we can even get out of bed, we need to know our purposes for being on this earth. I use the plural form because it's important to have different purposes for different parts of your life (a business purpose, a family purpose, an intrapersonal purpose) and because purposes change as time goes on. We like to consider purpose as something singular and innate, like personality, or soul. It's not. A purpose is a goal. As such, an entrepreneur should expect to have two or three purposes at a time and dozens throughout a lifetime. Purposes change as your life unfolds.

Having separate purposes for different parts of life creates the separation necessary to achieve work-life balance. When I'm with my family, I have a specific purpose with them, such as helping my daughter feel ready for the first day of high school, helping my son with his baseball pitching, or experiencing a family trip with as much depth as possible. Having objectives at home keeps me grounded and focused and bars work objectives from wheedling their way into my mind during family time.

Purposes will come and go as you achieve them. When Tiago was born, my purpose was to get him home from the hospital. Once he came home, my purpose was to alter the path the doctors had set for him and get Tiago to walk. Then that purpose changed to getting him out of his braces, then again to training for his first five-kilometer run at age twelve. You set a goal, and your purpose becomes to achieve that goal. I set a goal for one of my businesses, Kimurawear, to become the most distributed brand of boxing and martial arts equipment across Canada. Once we achieved that, I set a new purpose, to become the number-one choice for customizable equipment for gyms in Canada. We quickly achieved that goal.

Set your purposes. Expect to have several, and expect them to change. Only with a clear sense of your purposes can you begin to balance your schedule.

PRIORITIZE

Knowing your purposes, you must then order them by importance. Not everything should make the cut. There are only so many hours in the day, and a lot of them are for sleeping. The same way an entrepreneur triages prospective clients, so too must you triage your priorities.

I would suggest setting your purposes in this order: Good health comes first. Without our health, nothing else matters. Do you think a Porsche in the driveway will do you any good if you're lying in a hospital bed? Next comes loving family. Without loving family, you would have no one to enjoy your wealth with, and loneliness may be one of the saddest things anyone can endure. Third is success. I would classify this as financial, but success can also be measured by how many people you have touched or mentored.

What's more important? An hour a day to take care of your body—so you're healthier, happier, and live longer—or an extra hour to grow your business? Your nine-year-old daughter's dance recital—a once-in-a-lifetime event—or a business dinner you can bump to tomorrow? Based on your purposes, the choice of how to spend your time should be obvious. But you first have to recognize that the choice is even there.

When my daughter Sierra was little, before my son was born, I was that ultra-focused entrepreneur, the exact sort of individual I work so hard with now to teach the importance of balance. I was so focused on growing the business that I spent a lot of time on the road or working late nights in the office.

Though I didn't know it at the time, my priorities were all out of whack.

When you set the order of your priorities, health and family must always be on the top of our lists, no matter what. This is the natural order of things, and for good reason. If you don't have your health, you have nothing, so that must come first. You may have a brilliant mind for business and all the love in the world for your family, but if you're in poor health, you won't have the time or energy to take care of anything else.

After your health, family must be the most important thing. Business will always be there tomorrow; family might not. By bringing a child into the world, we make a promise to be there for that child. When we're not there, nothing else we do matters. I'm not going to try to convince you to make your children a priority. If you do not believe they should be, honestly, you should find another book.

Prioritizing is liberating. By taking care

of my health and making family my major priority, I've guaranteed I will always have quality time with my wife and kids, no matter how busy the workday may be. There is great peace in knowing that.

SET (AND STICK TO) YOUR SCHEDULE

When you're clear on your purposes and their order of priority, scheduling is easy. Start with your top priorities and build around them.

I structure my day to have a highly productive morning in order to make room for family time in the afternoon and evening. To achieve this, I wake up each day at 4:30 a.m. to 5:00 a.m. This is earlier than a lot of people are willing to get out of bed, but it gives me extra room for time with my family later in the day. This started by my waking up fifteen minutes earlier each day until I was waking up three hours earlier and getting three more hours with my family as a result. I'm not saying everyone needs to wake up at 4:30 a.m., but if growing your business and being with your family are high priorities for you, certain sacrifices are necessary to balance the two out.

First thing after waking up, I feed my dog and take a few minutes of quiet time to focus on my breathing and clear my mind, reflecting on the day past and the day ahead. Some call this meditation; others call it praying. I like to refer to it as quiet time. After that, I'll let the sun in, make myself a black coffee, take my vitamins, and spend five to ten minutes stretching and doing some form of a core workout (a stable core is critical for anyone who spends a large portion of his or her day behind a desk). Then I'll assemble a to-do list.

I still enjoy handwriting this to-do list. The night before, I will have emailed myself any lingering to-dos from the day before, and this is what I'll work from, with whatever I didn't accomplish the day before at the top of the next day's to-do list. From that list, I'll plot out the day ahead on my schedule, referring to my priorities when there's a conflict.

When you're building your schedule, it's important to remember that blank time can be just as valuable as scheduled time. This is a good window to catch up on priorities that may have fallen through the cracks. This may include calling your parents, replying to missed emails, or tending to an aspect of your health you've been thinking about less. Blank time is a powerful scheduling tool provided you are intentional about how you use it.

With my morning routine complete and the day scheduled in alignment with my priorities, I'll head to work. At 2:45 p.m., I'll leave the office, regardless of where my work stands. When that block of time is done, it's done. Respecting this boundary is critical for maintaining balance.

I've enshrined family time in my schedule from 3:00 p.m. to 7:00 p.m. Monday to Friday (and all day Sunday). Dinnertime, homework, sporting events, dance events, and family bike rides all tend to fall in this window. I've pre-blocked it, so there's no excuse for missing them. If taking those four hours to be with my family means getting up four hours earlier or staying up an hour later to make up for missed work, so be it. Family is my number-one purpose, so it is locked on my schedule.

After 7:00 p.m., if I need to be on a call or there's remaining work for the day, I'll step into my home office. I take extra care not to take work calls or answer work emails in my home environment. The entire point of prioritizing and scheduling my respective purposes is to keep them separated and balanced. Let them bleed into one another, and all that planning goes out the window.

A lot of people find it hard living such a highly scheduled life, but it's the price I pay for balancing family and entrepreneurship. And, of course, my schedule is never perfect.

It inevitably changes as the chaos of life runs its course. But entropy is not an excuse for living a disorganized life—just like gravity is no excuse for not exercising. Know your purposes, make them your priorities, and organize your schedule around them. Your future self, your family, and your business will thank you. I promise that.

The moment
you change
'I have to' into
'I get to,' your
life will become
wonderful.

CHAPTER 4

BE HOME FOR DINNER

FOR THE BUSY ENTREPRENEUR-DAD, dinnertime is a home run waiting to happen. It's a short, easy-to-schedule time block that gives you an opportunity to communicate and connect with your kids in a relaxed environment. Done right, it's delicious. Dinner with your family is a slow lob over the center of the plate. All you have to do is swing. Yet many fathers let the opportunity pass them by and strike out, caught looking.

PHONES AWAY

The ritual of family dinner has fallen out of favor in recent years. This is due in large part to the exponential development of technology and the rise of the all-important smartphone over the last two decades. The capabilities our phones give us are magnificent. Phones connect us and make us more powerful, but we must have times when we limit their use. Dinnertime is one of those times.

Before the benefits of a family meal can even enter the discussion, phones must be away. Making the time to have dinner together isn't worth a thing if no one's actually present. If someone goes onto his or her phone during a meal, that person has effectively left the dining room. If all those around the same table had their phones out, they might as well have eaten their meals on different continents. Phone apps hook into our dopamine-addicted brains and social media in particular has a spectacular ability to suck us in and keep us enthralled. Once we get sucked into a scroll session, we can get trapped in the social media world for hours without noticing that a five-minute check of the newsfeed turned into an hour and that dinnertime has come and gone.

TABLE SET

I grew up in a family where dinnertime held a position of unparalleled importance. We couldn't eat together every night because my dad often worked twelve-hour shifts, but when we did, it carried deep significance. My father had the choice of working weekends and getting paid for time and a half, but he chose not to so that he could focus on being with his family. Because he made that choice, our family got to have dinner together on the weekends.

Over dinner, we'd recap the week, with each of us taking a turn to share what ours had been like. It was a way for us all to know what was happening in one another's lives. As my sister and I grew up, our independence grew, but our sense of being part of a larger familial fabric never waned.

Because my parents had family dinner throughout my childhood, they established an open dialogue with me early and often. This way, when I stepped into the independence of adolescence, with all its dangers, the communication channels were wide open.

Many entrepreneur-dads only recognize the power of family dinner when their kids are older, and by then, it's often too late. As a parent of teenagers myself, I empathize with the desire to be sure children are safe and making the right decisions with the new autonomy of adolescence. A lot of parents realize when their kids become teenagers how having regular family dinners together would be one of the best ways to check in, but because their children are already so independent, they struggle to establish this pattern. Asking teenagers to take an hour out of each day to be with their family, during which their parents expect them to be vulnerable and honest, is a *tall* order. Asking little kids to do the same isn't half as difficult, and it enables them to have ongoing open dialogue with their parents down the road. The ritual of family dinner is a sacred time. It symbolizes togetherness. A family does not create such a symbol in a single night of food and conversation—though that can go a long way. It cultivates it over months and years. It's a habit. And like all good habits, the sooner you start, the better.

DIG IN

Food helps conversations flow. The simple act of eating helps us lower our guard and communicate honestly and with greater empathy. This is why business lunches and dinners are so important. A negotiation in a restaurant will be far more relaxed than one in an office, and both parties usually will leave feeling better about the end result.

Family dinners can create a space for free-flowing conversation, but they cannot make those conversations happen. If your ultimate goal is to achieve a greater understanding of what your children are going through, you have to lead a conversation where they feel comfortable opening up. To that end, there are two methods I've found useful in guiding dinnertime conversation.

First, speak from a place of honesty and vulnerability about what you're going through. It's not fair to expect your kids to open up about their day if you don't do the same with yours. Not only does this make it easier for everyone else around the table to be vulnerable, but it's also a great opportunity to create teaching moments.

When I tell my family about my day, I let it all hang out. If the world throws an adult-sized challenge my way, I tell my kids about it, warts and all. I'll even pepper in some curse words so they know I'm talking to them about real life. This way, when they face adult-sized challenges of their own, they won't be surprised, and they can call on a wealth of dinnertime lessons from Dad to help them rise to the occasion.

Second, to help the conversation flow and deepen, take the pressure off. Over time, expectations develop for what dinner is "supposed" to be like—we eat at this time, we talk this much, and we feel like this. Having some flexibility over what family dinners look like helps relieve this pressure. There is no "correct" way to have dinner with your family.

Once in a while, my family grabs takeout and has dinner in front of the TV. This is not the ideal dinner I've described throughout this chapter, and if we always ate this way, it might be a problem. But on occasion, it's a pleasant change of pace. The dog drools in our laps. The speakers fill the room with music and voices. We don't talk as much on those nights, but we're together. And when we eat together the next night, we're back around the table, deep in conversation.

At the end of the day, dinner is about togetherness. We might forget what we ate, where we were, or even what we spoke about, but we will not forget who was there. Eat together as a family, and the memory will last a lifetime.

Some of
the best
conversations
and memories
happen around
a meal.

CHAPTER 5

CREATE AND DOCUMENT MEMORIES

IT'S IMPORTANT TO TREAT a child's memory with intention and respect because the moments they record in their childhood will remain with them and shape who they are for the rest of their lives. To add to the challenge, the window for building up a bank of memories with your child is not long. Their childhood, despite how long it sometimes feels, is still very short.

There are two important components to cultivating a child's memories: making memories and recording them. Making a memory is like composing a picture. Who's there? What are they doing? What's the overall tone of the moment? Recording a memory is actually taking the picture, printing it, and saving it in a photo album.

Let's start with the first component, making memories.

MAKING MEMORIES: TWO TYPES

Most of the memories I make with my kids fall into one of two categories: Memories of their important moments (birthdays, graduations, performances) and memories I actively create for them (family trips, bike rides, special treats).

The first type of memory, being there for your child's important moments, is about diligence. Our children don't always seem to notice when we're there at an important moment of theirs. For example, my daughter has been training in dance since she was four, and as I write this, she dances on a high-performance competitive team. Over the ten years she's been dancing, my wife and I have taken her to all her classes, and we have never missed a recital. The likelihood that she'll remember every time I drove her to practice or every time I saw her perform is very low. However, when she looks back on her dance career, at the moments that were most important to her, she'll remember her dad was there.

We can never be sure what moments our kids will and will not remember. Be there for as many big ones as you can so you won't run the risk of missing something important.

The second category, memories you create for your child, is more of an artistic endeavor. It comes from who you are as a person and what you'd like to emphasize for your children. For me, physical health and challenging yourself are of great importance, so a lot of the moments I set to create memories with my kids reflect that. We go on bike rides. We do intense workouts. The actual content of these memories is up to fate, but the context is within our control, so I make sure our time together happens in a context I want my kids to remember.

There are, however, places where the two categories overlap, where the memories you create for your children also happen to be some of the more important moments in their lives. These are powerful memories. I have no formula to make such memories happen, but I can tell you this: a lot of the most important memories I've been able to create for my kids have happened on long, stinky drives.

HIGH-POTENCY MEMORIES: ROAD TRIPS

A year ago, my family went on a road trip to Myrtle Beach, South Carolina. For four days, we played and relaxed together in the sun, soaking up every minute. For the journey back, we'd prebooked a hotel in Virginia, halfway to our home in Toronto. The whole drive is about anywhere between fifteen to twenty hours, depending on amount of stops and our plan was to break it up into two days.

When it came time to leave, I looked at my wife and kids splashing in the ocean, and though we wouldn't make our hotel reservation, I couldn't do it. Everyone was having so much fun that I decided we should stay one more day in Myrtle Beach and knock out the return trip in one long day. And *long* it was.

After an extra day of fun on the beach, we packed the car and hit the road at 5:00 a.m. It was one of the hardest car rides of my life. My son threw up in the car twice, so everything smelled like barf. I almost hit a deer three times. Our bodies ached. Our stomachs hurt. It was awful.

But the memory of that car ride from hell is not awful at all—in fact, it makes us smile every time we think of it. To this day, we'll get in the car and laugh about it. "Remember when Tiago was throwing up and you almost hit that deer?" It's a memory we'll never forget.

Road trips are one of the best ways for a family to make memories together. It's an intimate experience, being huddled together for so many hours. You can't avoid learning about someone when you're trapped in close proximity that long. Sometimes it's pleasant—you sing songs together and have long heart-to-hearts. Sometimes it's not. People are going to argue. Smells are going to happen. Backs are going to get sore. All of these things, good and bad, make for rich memories.

The temptation to spend a family vacation relaxing at a resort is understandable. It's easier to sleep through a two hour and thirty minutes plane ride than drive for twenty hours. It's easier to order room service than it is to track down a roadside diner at 3:00 a.m. But when the trip is over, the memories of being at a resort are bland and less educational than those of being on a road trip. If all you're after is some time to relax, you might consider the former. But if your goal is to make memories with your family, you can do no better than an old-fashioned road trip. Just be sure to take lots of pictures and videos on the way.

DOCUMENT MEMORIES: PRINT YOUR PHOTOS

The second component of making memories with your kids is recording them. If you don't have some way of saving your memories with your kids, a lot of them will vanish with the passage of time. However, recording a memory is not as simple as snapping a photo, as our phones would have us believe. Taking a picture or video is one thing; actually looking at it later on is another.

In an age when most of us always have a camera at our fingertips, it has never been easier to take photos and videos, but it has also never been easier to lose them. Having them all stored electronically makes them vulnerable to getting erased, becoming destroyed, or, more often than not, simply being forgotten. For example, my family once went to Marineland in Niagara Falls, and while leaning over the black bear enclosure to take a photo, I dropped my phone—*plop*—into the water. It sank, never to be seen again, and a good number of family photos went with it. But even before I lost that phone, no one was looking at the pictures I had on it. My kids weren't gathering around the little screen, jostling for a better view. Those pictures were just sitting there, slowly fading from our memories.

This is why it's important to not only capture photos and videos, but to store them securely in a way your family can actually enjoy. Put your family movies on a private YouTube account or cloud storage so they're easy to share with one another. Connect your laptop to the TV or stream and play them on a big screen. Print your photos and store them in an album. Please, print your photos!

There is a quality to printed photos that makes us slow down and appreciate them in a way we don't with electronic photos. There's no logging in, scrolling through duplicates, pinching to zoom, or craning your neck to see. You can touch and hold a print. As the images age, the smell of the paper gets more special. The texture of the photo in your hands brings you back to that frozen moment in time. Everyone can gather around and look at it. More times than I can remember, I've gone upstairs to find my kids on the floor going through old photo albums, giggling, and reminiscing. I've never seen them do that around a phone.

Our photo album collections commemorate a special moment or period of our life, a certain trip or adventure, and bring strong memories of that specific occasion. When we scroll through photos on a phone, the images are scrambled as we keep adding on.

In addition to being easier to enjoy, physical copies of your memories are easier to pass down to future generations. Often, the photo albums my children enjoy most are from before they were born. The other day, my children were looking through photos of my dad from when he was eighteen years old and in the army. Their expressions were rapt. They asked their grandpa tons of questions: "What's that you're holding? What was it like? Why were you in the army?" They learned a lot about their grandfather, themselves, and the world that day—all because someone bothered to take those photos and store them in an album.

Memories are one of the few things we get to pass on to our children when we're gone.

There is little more human and important than that. Looking at pictures of their parents, grandparents, and those who came before them is a way for children to inherit pieces of their shared ancestral memory, which they can then pass down to their kids. It's a way to orient them to their family tree. But for that to happen, someone has to document those memories, store them, and share them.

Cherish
each moment.
We don't know
the value of
each moment
until it becomes
a memory.

CHAPTER 6

SET AND ACCOMPLISH GOALS TOGETHER

AN ENTREPRENEUR becomes successful by setting and accomplishing goals. When we do the same with our children, we give them the tools to achieve their own success while making valuable memories along the way. By ensuring they always have a meaningful objective they're working toward, we encourage them to strive upward. By holding them accountable to accomplishing the goals they set for themselves, we instill the values of hard work, discipline, and perseverance.

As entrepreneur-dads, we have an opportunity not every father has: the opportunity to teach our children the skills that helped us get ahead. There is, however, no way around the fact that those skills are hard-earned, and the path to success is difficult, complex, and, yes, painful. This is the first lesson we must impart when teaching our kids to set and accomplish goals for themselves. Achieving worthwhile goals is *hard*.

HELP BY NOT HELPING: CHALLENGE YOUR KIDS

No one likes watching their kids struggle. Most entrepreneur-dads have lived through challenging, even scary, years and don't want their kids to go through the same. They'd rather protect them, saying, "Dad's made it.

You guys don't have to worry about how to get ahead." This is a natural parental instinct with an important role to play in nurturing a child, but be wary. It's easy to take that protective urge too far, stunting a child's development.

There is perhaps no greater symbol of this than the participation trophy—an award just for showing up, praise for minimum effort. This is a dangerous precedent to set for a young person who's still learning self-motivation.

When my son was eleven, his baseball team (which I coached at the time) played in a tournament. The group was strong, boasting a 17-4 regular season record, and for the first two days of the tournament, that was how the boys played. However, in the final game of the tournament, against a team with a much worse record, the team put it in their heads that the game would be easy. They didn't try their hardest, and as a result, they lost. Given their skill level and the training they'd put in, they should've won the tournament. The scoreboard showed the game wasn't even close.

After our last game, the tournament organizers passed out silver trophies to the team. Getting second place in a hard-fought competition is a meaningful accomplishment, worth commemorating with an award. However, in this case, since the boys only came in second because they gave up on competing for first, their second-place trophies were essentially participation awards. Because I cared deeply about the team and its development, I told the players the honest truth. The team huddled up, each boy with a trophy in hand, and I told them, to their parents' horror, "This trophy means absolutely nothing. What happened today is nothing to be proud of."

A lot of the parents looked at me like I was crazy. Some of the kids sniffled. I felt mean and intense, like maybe I was being too harsh. But I wasn't. It was an act of loving kindness.

As their coach, my job was to help them become the best baseball players and people they could be. That day, they'd fallen short of their goal. If I had let them take that failure as an accomplishment that was memorialized as a trophy on their shelf, I'd have been allowing them to diminish their abilities. With that in mind, I doubled down and told them that once they were home, they should take that participation trophy outside and put it in the trash.

For an entrepreneur, there's no participation trophy. You don't gain anything for *trying* to have a business. There are no awards for mediocrity. True achievements only come through hard work and struggle, which are challenging concepts for a child to learn. Fortunately, as entrepreneurs, we are well versed in both, and we already have a framework through which we can impart to our kids this simple formula: set a goal, accomplish it, and repeat.

SETTING GOALS

Choosing an objective can be as hard as actually achieving one. This is especially true for children who are still developing their core identities and don't always know what they want. You know what I mean if you've floundered after being asked, "What do you want to be when you grow up?" If you don't set personal goals for your children, particularly when they're very young, there's a good chance they will simply go without.

There's a difference, however, between setting a goal for your child and imposing it on him or her. For an objective to be meaningful, it must start and end with who your child is. You might be the decision-maker who sets a goal for the child, but the initial reasons for that goal should come from within your child.

That being the case, the nature of your child should govern the goals you set together more than anything else. As a general guide, I've found two areas of life particularly powerful when setting goals for my children (and myself, for that matter):

The first and most important place I find goals that will be meaningful to my children is where their fears are. It might be riding a bike without training wheels. It might be speaking in front of a crowd. The actual fear itself is secondary; what's most important is the process of confronting it. Fear is not something we are born with. Fear is something that is implanted into us as children at a very young age by the ones we look up to. For instance, fear could be engraved in our minds by the memory of our parents yelling, "Don't touch that stove. You're going to burn your hand." Or maybe it was this: "Don't run down those stairs. You're going to fall." We might be carrying such memories forward as adults. This leads to fear—fear of failure or fear of what our family or peers will think, for instance. This all stops us as adults from achieving our true potential. By teaching my children to recognize their fears and then make the conscious decision to overcome them, I've set them up to not be afraid when life gets *really* scary. They understand fear is something to conquer head-on.

Second, I recommend all entrepreneur-dads set fitness goals for their children and themselves. Many entrepreneurs struggle to maintain a healthy lifestyle through the anxiety and chaos of their work, which in turn sets a bad example for their kids. It's not fair to expect your child to take care of his or her body if you don't do the same. Set a fitness goal for yourself. Set one for your kid. Ideally, set one you can work on together.

When you're working toward a physical goal with your kid, you're really meeting three objectives with one simple and healthy solution: You're spending time together, you're instilling the value of a healthy lifestyle in your child, and you're keeping yourself physically fit. All three pay dividends down the road. A child with a healthy lifestyle will be far more likely to have a healthy lifestyle in adulthood. If you're healthier, you'll probably live to see more of that adulthood. And the memories you make exercising together will last a lifetime, maybe longer (remember to take photos).

Right now, my kids and I are training for a five-kilometer run. It's challenging, and after the first two kilometers, we all start to ache. But after our workouts, my kids and I feel fantastic. We are bonding over our shared discomfort, the endorphins are pumping, and we're that much closer to achieving our goal. Once we've run the race, we'll carry the memory of that accomplishment for the rest of our lives. Perhaps in thirty years, my son will show his children a picture of us crossing the finish line and inspire them to take on a physical challenge of their own.

ACCOMPLISHING GOALS

It's important for children to understand that once they've set out to accomplish a goal, they shouldn't stop until they've reached it. When people set goals, they make a commitment to themselves. It's OK to fail in pursuit of that goal—in fact; it's often the only way to learn how to achieve it. It's not OK, however, to give up. If children abandon a goal, they've broken a promise, which we as parents must refuse to accept. It's up to us to hold them accountable.

Sometimes, keeping my kids in line with their goals means making them do things they don't want to do. This strictness can sometimes leave you feeling kind of mean— the same way I felt telling my son's baseball team the truth about their trophies. When this doubt sets in, I think forward to how my child will feel after reaching a goal and the lifelong memories and skills to be gained, and I recognize that holding the child accountable is an act of love.

The best trick I've found for keeping my kids accountable is to do whatever it is that needs doing with them. If I tell my daughter to run forty flights of stairs, I lace up my sneakers and run them with her. At work, I lead my team by example, and I never ask anyone to do something I wouldn't be willing to do myself. It makes sense that I should lead my children by the same standard.

As entrepreneurs, we have a wealth of skills to impart to our children that will give them an advantage throughout their lives. There is perhaps no greater skill, however, than the ability to set and accomplish goals. When we teach our children this skill, we receive innumerable memories and lessons in return, but more than that, we set them up for a lifetime of achievement. Already my kids are blowing me away with their accomplishments. I can't wait to see where they'll go next.

Pursuing
goals creates
the road trips
between dreams
and success.

CHAPTER 7

GUIDE YOUR CHILDREN TO FIND THEIR OWN PATH

NOT FAR FROM MY HOME, there's a small town with these vintage brick-and-mortar storefronts that have signs with family names atop their front windows. As you read this, you're probably not far from a business with a family name. They're everywhere. The concept of children taking over their parents' businesses is embedded in our culture.

It's a sweet idea, children carrying on their parents' legacy in such a tangible way. Admittedly, part of me hopes one of my kids will choose to do so with one of my businesses (though I'm not holding my breath). There is nothing wrong with hoping your kids will follow your path. There is, however, a lot wrong with expecting them to.

THE BURDEN OF EXPECTATION

An entrepreneur recently told a story on my podcast about the burden of his father's expectations. The details were new, but the plotline was one I'd heard dozens of times before. Indeed, in my own mild way, I'd lived it. Growing up, this entrepreneur had his father tell him he was going to take over the family business. Not that he *could* take it over—that he was *going to*. When he was fourteen, he started learning the ins and outs of the organization, and as a young adult, he took it over, despite his own desires and ambitions. With no interest in the business or his work, he grew depressed and became an alcoholic. Years later, he got his personal life back on track and went to rehab, but only after the family business was sold was he able to focus on his own career and his true passion of coaching others.

I could slightly relate. While my dad didn't expect me to follow in his footsteps, he did push for me to follow a path that would lead to a secure career. He thought I would make a great police officer. I started down that path even though my entrepreneurial journey had already begun. I got as far as a college course on police foundations before I realized that I really wanted to focus on being my own boss. I was truly lucky to have a family that supported me once I got this clarity on my future path.

Unsurprisingly, neither the entrepreneur on my podcast nor I found true happiness until we untethered ourselves from others' expectations and found our own way forward.

As entrepreneur-dads, we have to be careful not to set expectations for the future of our children. What we can do is help them focus on their strengths and help guide them toward the best path for success. As parents, we all want the best for our children's future. Providing them with all the tools and guidance necessary to achieve their own personal goals should be our goal.

BUILD THEIR SELF-BELIEF

Often when starting a new business, entrepreneurs come to a point where everything tells them they're wrong. The ideas aren't there. The market isn't ready. You can't do this. What separates entrepreneurs from would-be entrepreneurs; it is the ability to push past these doubts and believe in themselves, which can take unflagging self-belief. There is no greater belief we can teach our children than this.

Above each of my kids' bedrooms hangs a hand-carved wooden sign that reads, "Believe in yourself." Every night when they go to bed, whether the day was good or bad, one of the last things they see is that message. It's a message I reiterate at every opportunity, to the point where it's almost a catchphrase. Believe in yourself. Believe in yourself. *Believe in yourself.*

As big decisions arise for my kids—whether or not to go to college, what sort of career to build, when is the right time to start a family— they will have to look within themselves for the answer. I can offer my own experiences as lessons. I can be a sounding board for their ideas and offer emotional support. But only they can make the decision. There's no piece of advice I can give that will serve them better than their own self-confidence. Part of this is helping your kids overcome their fears. Every entrepreneur knows that it's hard to feel confident when you're afraid.

My daughter wanted to enter a public speaking competition at school, but fear was holding her back from entering. In the weeks leading up to the event, we focused on building her self-confidence by having her practice her speech in front of my wife and me. She entered, won her class, grade, and school, and went on to place fifth out of 1,750 students in the district competition. Needless to say, she's a brilliant speaker, but without the confidence to enter the competition in the first place, she would have never entered and let this goal of hers slip away.

This is why it's so important for children to learn to believe in themselves early on. Without a strong sense of confidence, people tend to be too risk averse, allowing things like self-doubt and uncertainty to undermine their aspirations. This leads many onto the path of least resistance, where dreams go to die. When people believe in themselves, they have the self-assuredness to take the risks they need to take in pursuit of their passion. This, in turn, helps create their purpose. Passion and purpose go hand in hand. Without a true passion, the end purpose has no meaning, and the drive to achieve that purpose will disappear.

FOLLOW THEIR LEAD: HOW TO HELP CHILDREN FIND THEIR BLISS

We all can be a Michael Jordan, Steve Jobs, or Oprah Winfrey at one particular thing that we truly have a passion for. All people have at least one thing they're capable of becoming exceptional at, but it's not always easy to find. Many go their whole lives without knowing what they're really good at, or they only discover it when it's too late. For this reason, it's critical that we help our children figure out what their natural gifts are, starting at a young age. From there, we can give them little nudges toward their talents so that they can see for themselves which areas they're most passionate about.

Encouraging our children to explore their natural inclinations is not the same, however, as pigeonholing them into a set path. That's no better than expecting them to take over the family business. We have to understand that their passions can and will change as they grow up.

For instance, my daughter does high-performance dance. To nurture this pursuit, my wife and I have done everything in our power to surround Sierra with top instructors, equipment, and talent to allow her to achieve her highest level. Does this mean we expect her to be a professional dancer? Of course not.

She's also a natural entrepreneur and passionate about animals. To support her in exploring these strengths, I helped her draw up plans for a doggy daycare business. As parents, we have set up saving accounts for both our children to one day start up their own businesses or proceed to the college route—whatever path they choose to follow.

Do I expect either to go to college? Or be entrepreneurs? Not at all. All I'm doing is helping them explore different paths and giving them their best opportunities. As they get older, they will gravitate toward what they are most passionate about.

Whom a child spends his or her time with will help or hinder this gravitation. As a coach for entrepreneurs, I encourage all to surround themselves with a least five people they aspire to be like or who are at their level and add value to their lives. This same thinking should be taught to our children. They will emulate the company they keep. If they surround themselves with passionate, driven individuals, they are likely to be passionate and driven themselves. If they surround themselves with losers, well—you get the picture. As a parent, it's important to know who your child's five closest friends are and, as much as possible, help your child select a crowd that enriches the child's life and challenges the child to grow.

With or without our help, our children are going to determine their own path. By guiding them toward their natural tendencies, we can make that journey of self-discovery easier and more fruitful, but we have to pay close attention to how those tendencies change over time. It's kind of like a dance, where you follow your child's lead. The key is a steady hand and a loose grip. Let them show you where they want to go on the dance floor and provide unwavering support as they find their rhythm.

As a father
you set strong
family roots;
then you give
your children
wings.

A man who views the world the same at fifty as he did at twenty has wasted thirty years of his life.

—Muhammad Ali

ABOUT
THE AUTHOR

JEFF LOPES IS A PROUD FATHER of two, a husband, and a serial entrepreneur for the past twenty four years Jeff has built numerous companies from the inception to 7 and 8 figure corporations, including TrueBlue Homes, a portfolio of vacation rentals properties across the northern parts of Ontario, Canada and Kimurawear a boxing and martial arts equipment brand that was incepted in early 2006 out of his home basement. Jeff is currently a host of a top-rated entrepreneurial podcast Jeff

Knows Inc Show. Over the past three years, Jeff has coached countless entrepreneurs in balancing the challenges of fatherhood and entrepreneurship and achieving a great level of success in both. As Fitness Leadership College Graduate and certified NLP Master & Life Coach, Jeff has taken all his experiences to create Mans Purpose™, a brotherhood for Entrepreneur-Dads. This membership-based platform was designed to lead men on creating a higher purpose within themselves physically, mentally and spiritually. This will lead to greater levels of success within their business, creating financial freedom and giving an opportunity for these men to become more present and active, as fathers and partners. He lives and works in Toronto, Canada with his wife, Lucy, two children, Sierra and Tiago, and a chocolate lab named Jax.

www.ingramcontent.com/pod-product-compliance
Lightning Source LLC
Chambersburg PA
CBHW070941210326
41520CB00021B/6995

* 9 7 8 1 6 4 7 7 5 2 8 1 1 *